chinchilla

understanding and caring
for your pet

Written by
Dr Anne McBride BSc PhD Cert.Cons FRSA

Additional Material:
Donna Bean
chinchillas4life.co.uk

chinchilla

understanding and caring
for your pet

Written by
Dr Anne McBride BSc PhD Cert.Cons FRSA

Additional Material:
Donna Bean
chinchillas4life.co.uk

Magnet & Steel Ltd

www.magnetsteel.com

Printed and bound in China through Printworks International.

ISBN: 978-1-907337-22-2
ISBN: 1-907337-22-9

Contents

Perfect pets

Chinchillas, with their plush fur coats, bright eyes and lively character, have become increasingly popular as pets. They come in a variety of colours and are small creatures, with both males and females weighing around 600g (1.3lb).

They are very sensitive and yet have a lively nature, but they can be injured easily if they are handled roughly or frightened. Therefore they are not suitable pets for young children. However, chinchillas can provide a lot of pleasure to the dedicated owner.

These are reasons why chinchillas are attractive animals to keep.

- If treated gently, they are friendly animals and enjoy being stroked by their owners

- Chinchillas usually live for 15 to 20 years and sometimes longer.

- They are not expensive to buy and, once you have bought your initial equipment, they are relatively cheap to feed and house compared to a cat or dog.

Opposite: Children, especially young children should be supervised at all times when with there chinchillas.

- However, be aware that appropriate accommodation may cost hundreds of pounds and costs of feed and veterinary fees, such as neutering, must be factored into your decision to obtain chinchillas as pets.

- Chinchillas are particularly beautiful and appealing animals with their large eyes, rounded ears and heads and a dense coat of velvet-like fur.

However, you need to be aware of the following facts.

- Chinchillas can be susceptible to dental problems; which can prove to be very expensive as they will require lifelong treatment. You may want to take out insurance against veterinary fees.

- They do not tolerate wide temperature changes, damp or humid conditions. They need to be kept as indoor pets. They can suffer from cold and heatstroke and need to be kept in a temperature range of 16 to 25C (61 to 77F), in low humidity and free from draughts. They cannot be kept outside in the UK or other temperate regions as the atmosphere is too humid and the range of temperature is too great.

- Chinchillas are very active animals and need to be kept in suitably-sized accommodation. They are most active between dusk and dawn – that is overnight, in the evening and in the early morning.

As indoor pets, chinchillas can be quite noisy at night as they explore their cage, and play with their toys.

Pictured: Two is company. Chinchillas are sociable animals.

- They are sociable animals and ideally should be kept in pairs.

Some people are allergic to the fur of animals and may suffer health problems if a pet is kept in the house. Your doctor can test for this, and this is worth doing before you consider buying chinchillas as pets.

Special
needs

Like all animals, chinchillas have their own special requirements, regarding food, companionship and accommodation, which you need to know about before buying them. This is important so you can enjoy a good relationship with your chinchillas, and they can live long, healthy and happy lives. Under the UK Animal Welfare Act (2006) you now have a legal obligation to ensure your pets are healthy, properly cared for and happy.

You will need to handle your chinchillas very gently as they are easily frightened, especially when picked up. If they try to escape a person's hands they may lose part of their fur or even the skin off their tail.

Opposite: Let your chinchilla come to you.

Chinchillas also have small, fragile bones, which are easily damaged.

Your chinchillas need the right food to stay fit and healthy. They have a special requirement for high fibre food.

You will need to clean out your chinchillas' home frequently, and provide a large, safe area where your chinchillas can exercise every evening and night outside their cage/sleeping area. Ideally, they should have constant access to this exercise area so they can run around when they choose.

You should also provide special features in your chinchillas' home, so they can exercise, climb, hide and dust bathe daily.

You will need to make arrangements for someone to look after your chinchillas if you go away on holiday.

Register your chinchillas with a veterinary practice, and remember they should visit the vet at least once a year to have their teeth checked.

Check your chinchillas' coat, weight, teeth and nails every week and commit to looking after your pets throughout their long lives.

What is a Chinchilla?

Wild Ancestors

The wild ancestors of all our pet chinchillas come from South America, in particular the arid slopes of the central Andes mountains, where they live at altitudes of up to 5000 metres (16,400 feet). Pet chinchillas share the same basic behaviours as their wild cousins, so it is useful to know about how chinchillas live in the wild.

Chinchillas are members of the order Rodentia. Rodents are the biggest group of mammals and make up about half of all known mammal species. There are some 2000 different species of rodents, ranging in size from the tiny harvest mouse, weighing only 7g (less than a third of an ounce), to squirrels and beavers.

Pictured: Chinchillas have a rounded body, bright eyes and a beautiful coat.

The largest is the Capybara, which can grow to a metre long (3 feet) and weigh 60 kilos (132 lb).

The word rodent comes from the Latin word 'rodere', which means to gnaw, and gnawing is one thing all rodents have in common. They gnaw to get their food and, in the case of the beaver, to make their homes. Rodents have four big front teeth, the incisors, which have evolved for gnawing. They are sharp and chisel-shaped and meet together like pincers. The teeth of all rodents grow continually throughout the animal's life.

Chinchillas belong to a small family of rodents known as the chinchillidae, which consists of two species of chinchillas and five species of viscachas, their close cousins.

The word chinchilla means 'little Chincha', the Chincha being a native tribe who wore chinchilla fur. The chinchilla species are the *C. lanigera*, which literally means the woolly chinchilla, but is commonly known as the long-tailed chinchilla, and *C. brevicaudata*, which translates as the short-tailed chinchilla. Unfortunately, wild chinchillas are now extremely rare, and it is thought that the short-tailed chinchilla may be extinct, as it has not been seen in the wild since 1953.

Opposite: A comfy place to sit.

Wild chinchillas are hunted illegally for their fur, and appropriate habitat is vanishing fast due to livestock grazing and mining activities.

The chinchilla is now listed as critically endangered by the IUCN (International Union for the Conservation of Nature). If you are interested in finding out more about wild chinchillas, and how you can help, then see the further reading section.

The natural home of the chinchilla is high up on the dry, rocky slopes of the Andes in Chile, Bolivia and Peru. Their home is arid, and has semi-desert conditions in terms of humidity. It can be cold in the winter, and is never very hot, even at the height of summer. Thus it is important that animals in this environment can keep warm and conserve their body fluids.

Chinchilla bodies are superbly adapted to this environment. First, their coat is dense and soft, enabling them to keep warm and prevent loss of body fluid from the skin. They do not sweat, but produce concentrated urine and small dry faeces, further ensuring loss of body fluid is kept to a minimum.

Food in the wild is not always available in the same place, and different foods will be around at different times of year, depending on whether it is the wet or dry season. This means chinchillas have evolved as animals that can eat a range of plants as they become available.

Chinchillas are opportunistic herbivores. They do not eat meat of any kind.

Sources of drinking water also fluctuate and may not exist in the dry season. In the wild they rarely drink, but obtain their fluids from the evening and morning dew on the fresh plants and grasses that they eat, and the moisture in the vegetation itself. Chinchillas are particularly appealing when they eat, as they sit up, as if at an invisible table, holding their food in their front paws and delicately nibble away.

The foods available in the wild include grasses, cacti, cacti fruit and evergreen shrubs. This vegetation is full of fibre, coarse to eat and not particularly nutritious. The Chinchilla is very well adapted to such a diet with its continuously growing teeth and special digestive system.

Chinchillas need lots of fibre in their diet to keep their gut healthy and, like rabbits, they are caecotrophic. This means they basically digest their food twice. The first time the food passes through the gut it comes out in soft, caecal pellets which the chinchilla picks up, chews and swallows.

The second time it passes through the gut it is re-digested to extract all the nutrition available, leaving only the non-nutritious portions to be excreted as hard pellets.

Chinchillas live in groups known as herds or colonies. Depending on the supply of food and number of safe places, there may only be a few individuals or a couple of hundred or more in a group. The actual social structure of the herd is not really understood, but there does seem to be some degree of hierarchy, with younger animals deferring to older ones by acknowledging their seniors with a high-pitched call when they meet.

It is important to realise that chinchillas are prey animals and are a major source of food for meat-eating animals (predators) in their natural environment. As they live so high in the mountains there are few land predators, though mountain lions and weasels are native to the Andes, and red foxes are a more recent addition.

The main enemy are large birds, such as condors and owls. This means that all chinchillas are continuously on the lookout for danger. Living in a herd not only provides companionship, but also the safety of many sets of ears, eyes and noses, all acting as early warning systems against predators, thus increasing the chance of escape.

If a predator is seen, a loud alarm bark is given and all the chinchillas will run to the safety of rock crevices or the short burrows that they have dug.

Chinchillas are extremely agile and active creatures. Their long back legs enable them to perform amazing athletic feats. They can jump up to 1.8m (6ft) in a single bound, and even vertically, using their long, flexible tail as a rudder.

Being able to move and jump quickly helps them escape from predators, but if they are caught, they have a couple more tricks. First, they can literally slip fur from their body, or if caught by their tail they can 'de-glove' it. This means that both fur and skin slips off the tail. Both are extreme defences, but do mean the chinchilla may survive.

De-gloving leaves the chinchilla with only the muscle and bone on the de-gloved part of the tail, which is then clearly exposed to the possibility of infection. But chinchillas are fastidiously clean animals and the very dry climate means most will grow back the skin and fur. Any part of the tail that is really damaged will dry out and simply fall off.

Chinchillas spend their nights foraging for food, resting with their companions, grooming each other, exploring (they are very curious creatures) and defending their home from other chinchilla groups.

As plants are available at different times in different places, chinchilla home ranges vary in size in the wild depending on what foods are growing nearby.

The home of a colony may be as much as 113 hectares (285 acres) or as small as 1.5 hectares (3.75 acres). Larger, conspicuous rocks are used as lookout posts and also as latrine (group toilet) sites, which advertise the territory boundary to other groups of chinchillas.

Chinchillas spend the days keeping cool and safely hidden away from predators while they catch up on their sleep and eat their caecal pellets. They make simple burrows underground that are narrow but open out into a wider 'room' at the end, or they shelter in rock crevices or even inside certain types of plants known as bromeliads.

This natural behaviour needs to be considered when providing accommodation for your pet chinchillas. They need shelter, and sufficient space to be able to run, jump, dust bathe, dig and forage every day/night when they choose. Chinchillas are social animals and research has shown that they need to have at least one other chinchilla companion.

Courtship happens in the late winter and early spring, and the male will follow the female, gently nibbling her fur.

Opposite: Chinchillas are active and curious creatures.

However, if she does not want his attentions, she may get feisty. A female may leap in the air to box an unwanted suitor with her hind feet, or spray him with urine!

Pregnancy lasts just over three months. The room in the burrow may be lined with soft grasses for the birth, though mother and young will leave the nest within a few hours. Though there may be up to six offspring born, a more usual litter size is only one or two. Wild chinchillas usually have two litters a year, as the female will often become pregnant again within a day of giving birth.

Many of the animals we keep as pets, such as dogs, cats and rabbits have young that are born blind, deaf and furless, known as altricial young. However, baby chinchillas are precocial – that is, they are born looking like miniature adults, as are guinea pigs, sheep, cows and horses.

Baby chinchillas are called kits. At birth their eyes are open, they have a full set of teeth, are furry and are able to walk around and keep up with their mother within an hour of being born. This is important, because the group may have to move location if there is limited food and the youngsters must be able to follow, and be able to escape predators by running away.

Baby chinchillas are not weaned until six to eight weeks after birth, though they can survive without their mother's milk after only a month, and will start to nibble food when they are about a week old. They will learn which plants are good to eat from the taste of their mother's milk, and by watching what the adults eat. This is important, as the chinchilla has to be versatile because the harsh environment means that the same food is unlikely to be available all year round.

Both the parents take part in the rearing of their young, grooming and playing with them. Young chinchillas are very inquisitive and playful. Play comprises of hopping, jumping vertically, twisting and generally racing around. If the kits are too boisterous they will be 'told off' by an adult making a grunting sound, and the youngsters show respect to their parents by making a high-pitched noise. The family will sleep huddled close together while the kits are young.

The kits are weaned when they are about two months old. The males become sexually mature around six months of age and the females at eight months. At this time they will have developed their adult coat which, whilst extremely beautiful, sadly was the undoing of the species as it brought chinchillas firmly to the notice of Westerners.

Opposite: Baby chinchillas are born fully furred.

The human link

For several hundred, if not thousands, of years chinchillas and humans lived in harmony. Chinchillas were hunted by native South American Indians for food and fur, but this hunting was in balance with the environment. That is, the people never took more than they needed, and never more than the chinchilla population could withstand.

However all that changed with the arrival of the Spanish in the early 16th century. Within 50 years, the Spanish had conquered and settled much of the South American continent and had taken chinchilla pelts back to Europe. The beauty and rarity of the chinchilla fur meant that, for the next 200 years or so, it was worn only by European royalty and the very wealthy.

Opposite: Hold your chinchilla gently but firmly.

However, the demand for the fur spread across Europe and, increasingly, more chinchillas were hunted. It takes the pelts from 100 - 150 chinchillas to make a single fur coat, and many thousands of fur coats, collars and gloves were wanted.

Indeed, in the 1800s chinchilla fur was one of the top three exports of South America. This indiscriminate over-hunting had a disastrous effect on the numbers of wild chinchillas. The situation was exacerbated by the extensive mining for minerals such as copper, silver and gold in the Andes by many countries, including the British. Not only did mining destroy chinchilla habitat, but the British also introduced the fox to the area which added another predator and put more pressure on the fragile chinchilla population.

By the 1890s chinchillas were on the verge of extinction. Indeed, the situation was so bad that in 1918 the governments of Bolivia, Chile and Peru banned both the hunting of chinchillas and the export of their pelts, though sadly illegal hunting did, and still does, continue.

A year later, in 1919, an American, Mathias Chapman, who had been working for the mining industry, obtained permission from the Chilean government to collect live chinchillas to take to California, where he wanted to breed them.

Opposite: Chinchillas are always alert to danger.

It took him nearly three years to collect 11 specimens good enough to breed from, and these are the ancestors of the millions of chinchillas that have been bred around the world for the fur and pet trade since.

In California, Chapman soon built up a herd of animals and sold the offspring to other farmers. These early animals cost as much as £1,000 a pair, but over the following 50 years many thousands of chinchilla fur farms were set up all over the world and chinchilla fur became progressively cheaper and available to more people.

But fashions change and after the Second World War new materials were available for clothing, including warm winter clothing. There was also an increase in our understanding of, and respect for, animals, which led to the wearing of fur becoming less popular. By 1960s the demand for fur had started to diminish, so breeders and fur farmers started to sell chinchillas as pets.

Over the years, breeders found that through genetic mutations different coat colours would appear in their herds. These were sometimes radically different from the original wild type colouration, and were not very useful for the fur trade, which wanted to make coats and gloves that matched.

However, when chinchillas started to be sold as pets, owners were attracted to these unusual colours and patterns and they have become increasingly popular ever since.

Chinchilla Fur Breeders Association was set up in the UK, which later became, in 1993, the National Chinchilla Society. No longer associated with the fur trade, it is the UK society for those wishing to show their chinchillas. The Mutation Chinchilla Breeders Association is the American equivalent.

The chinchilla's world

This section describes how chinchillas experience the world.

Nose

The amount of twitching of the nose and whiskers shows how important the sense of smell is to a chinchilla. He relies on smell to find the best food, to avoid poisonous plants, to detect the scent of a nearby predator and to recognise other individual chinchillas, or humans.

Whiskers

Chinchilla whiskers are longer than the width of his body for a very good reason. The whiskers are used for touch, to help the animal find his way in the dark. Most specifically, the whiskers enable the chinchilla to measure the width of tunnels and crevices.

If the chinchilla can get his whiskers through a hole, he can get his body through too – a point worth remembering if you are letting your pets out and about in your home!

Mouth

The chinchilla's tongue and sensitive lips are used to test if items can be eaten.

Teeth

The chinchilla's 20 teeth grow all the time, as the natural foods they eat are coarse and wear down the teeth. The incisors at the front grow more rapidly than the molars at the back. The incisors grow about 1.5 mm (0.06 inches) a week – approximately 8cm (3 inches) in a year. This is why a constant supply of good quality hay is essential to prevent dental problems, in particular overgrown and mis-shaped (mal-occluded) teeth (see Health section). In addition, chinchillas need hard objects to gnaw on, such as pumice stone or untreated pieces of wood such as willow and fruit trees (except plum and cherry).

Eyes

Chinchilla eyes are on the side of the head, just above the mid-line. This means they can see behind them, to the sides and above, which helps them to detect predators such as a bird of prey.

As they are mostly active when the light is low, they have very good night vision, and can detect slight movements at a distance.

Unlike many nocturnal rodents, such as mice and rats, the iris of a chinchilla's eye is heavily pigmented, giving it a natural deep, rich, dark colour. The pupil is a vertical slit, rather like a cat's. These adaptations mean they can tolerate light better than many of their nocturnal cousins and can enjoy basking in the sunlight of the late evening and early morning.

All mammals have a blind spot where they cannot see. In a human these are above and behind the head; for chinchillas, it is in front of their noses. Remember this and try to move your hand towards them from the side, so as not to startle them.

Ears

The chinchilla's range of hearing is very similar to that of humans, but more acute, which means they can hear sounds at much lower volumes than we can. This is very important if they are going to have enough warning of a predator to get away to safety. Their ears are large and upright to help catch slight sounds from far away.

Body

Chinchillas have a rounded, compact shape, which helps them keep warm. Their thick coat makes them look bigger and more solid than they actually are. In reality, they are quite fragile creatures with light bones.

Feet

Chinchilla feet have four toes and bare soles, which they use to grip as they climb and clamber. Like the rest of the chinchilla, the toes are fragile and can easily be broken, for example if they get caught in the wire mesh of the cage.

Front legs

These are short with very flexible toes that the chinchilla can use for grasping food or rocks as he climbs, and balance as he moves. The front feet are used in much the same way as we use our hands.

Hind legs

The hind legs are longer than the front legs and are powerful. They enable the chinchilla to move very fast, using a kangaroo-like gait. They also act as launch pads propelling the chinchilla to heights of a metre (3ft) and distances of nearly two metres (6ft).

Tail

The tail of the chinchilla is striking. It is between 15 and 20cm (6-8in) long and bushy, with long, coarse hair. The tail is an essential balancing aid, enabling the chinchilla to climb steep, rocky areas in his native habitat and to lean over edges without falling off!! Chinchillas use their tail to balance when they sit up on their hind legs, giving them more height to look for any danger. They also use their tail to send messages to each other (see behaviour section).

Coat

The coat of the chinchilla is his most famous characteristic. It is soft and uniquely dense. Unlike other animals, chinchillas have many hairs growing from a single follicle. Where we only have one, a chinchilla has on average 75 hairs and maybe as many as 120! This means they shed their coat in tufts, and can do so if caught by a predator, which may simply end up with a mouthful of fluff as the chinchilla rushes away.

The Chinchilla coat has two types of hair. The bristle hairs are slightly longer and stiffer, growing 20 to 40mm (0.8 – 1.6in) long. Under these outer hairs are the softer brush hairs that give the plush feel to the coat and keep the chinchilla warm.

The chinchilla gets his adult coat when he is about nine months old, and will have his first moult at a year. This will then happen annually for the rest of his life.

The thick coat is very difficult for parasites such as fleas and ticks to penetrate, and chinchilla rarely suffer from these. The hairs however, are easily damaged and thus it is advised that chinchilla are not brushed. So long as they have frequent access to a dust bath, their coat will remain clean and healthy.

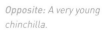

Opposite: A very young chinchilla.

Colours

Chinchillas come in a range of colours. Many are self-explanatory, but the list below will help you understand a selection of the more common terms. In the chinchilla show world, colours are further subdivided into categories relating to the depth of colour by terms such as light, medium, dark and extra dark. These colours, as with other species, are due to genetic mutations from the original wild colour. These mutations are selected by breeders who will mate particular individuals together to produce offspring of a desired colour.

Standard Grey (UK) Naturalle (USA)

Pictured: Standard Grey.

This is the natural, wild colour of the chinchilla, and the one so desired by the original fur trade.

It is such a famous colour that it is often used to describe a similar colour in other animals such as 'chinchilla' coloured cats and rabbits.

The natural colour of chinchillas is a pearly blue-grey. This is due to the bands of colour on the individual hairs. Near the skin the hairs are a dark grey, along the middle they are a lighter colour, returning to the dark shade at the tip of the hair. The fur of the chinchilla's belly is a pale blue-white. This contrast of darker top and pale belly is known as the agouti pattern and is common in many wild animals, such as rabbits.

Black

This colour is not quite as you may first think. The black colour lies as a cape or mantle across the head, neck and back, while the sides are grey and the belly a clear white.

The other colours of chinchilla are characterised by the loss of the agouti pattern and the colour being evenly distributed over the body.

Charcoal or Ebony

These can range from a deep black colour to a charcoal grey, reminiscent of the standard. However, in this colour category, the distinctive banding of the standard coat is missing.

Beige

These range from a darker brown and tan colour to a pale brown. The eyes of the lighter forms tend to be pink or ruby red in colour.

White

As it suggests, these chinchillas are white in colour, with ruby eyes. They can also have different shades, such as silver, or different patterns such as beige on the head or body.

Above:
Black
Below:
White

Sapphire

These chinchillas have a light blue undercoat with a blue bar midway up the hairs. The ears are pink and the tail has a pale sapphire colour to it.

Violet

The violet or lavender colour comes from the pale purple-blue undercoat and bar part way up the hairs, which subtly contrasts with the white belly fur.

Above:
Sapphire
Below:
Violet

One chinchilla or two?

Chinchillas are social animals and it is strongly recommended that you have two, so that when you are not able to spend time with them, they will not be lonely. The most successful arrangement is to have a neutered male and a female. Neutering will mean that you will not have unexpected baby chinchillas which you may not be able to find good homes for.

Female chinchillas will usually live together with little friction, especially if they have known each other since they were young. Two males can also live together, providing their are no females around.

Pictured: Chinchillas are happier with company.

However, when they reach sexual maturity (around 7 months) two males may fight for dominance, even if they have known each other all their lives.

If you currently only have one chinchilla, you should consider getting it a companion. However, adult chinchillas do not accept new cage mates easily. If your chinchilla has lived on his own for a long time he may not welcome another. In that case, you must make sure your chinchilla gets plenty of attention from you, every day. You may also wish to contact a reputable chinchilla rescue to see if they can find your chinchilla a companion and introduce them appropriately.

Introducing a new companion is never easy, but it is worth trying rather than keeping a solitary chinchilla.

Setting up home

Before you buy your chinchillas, you will need to decide where you are going to keep them and then buy suitable housing. Though chinchillas tolerate, and appreciate cooler accommodation, they cannot cope with damp or humid air. As a consequence they can only be kept as indoor pets in most places, including throughout all of the UK.

They usually tolerate cooler conditions better than hot ones, and the ideal temperature range is 16–18C (61–64F). Accommodation should be well ventilated but not draughty, be in the shade, and located away from sunny windows or radiators. Indeed, on sunny days it is advisable to draw the curtains or blinds so the room stays cool.

Opposite: I can see, hear and smell you.

Chinchillas are extremely susceptible to heatstroke if the temperature exceeds 24C (75F). This is even more of a problem if the air is humid.

Ensure your chinchillas have plenty of water to drink. You can wrap a metal bottle filled with iced water in a towel, which you can place so the chinchillas can lie next to it to stay cool, or buy a chinchilla 'ice hammock'. Providing tiling slabs for your chinchillas to lie on, or a deep bedding of sand in a box, will also help keep them cool.

The chinchillas' home must have a safe sleeping area as part of larger accommodation that includes an exercise area which they can access at will. You may also have an additional safe area where they can go free in your home, under supervision.

Ideally, your chinchillas' home should be as large as possible, and have toys and a sand pit so these intelligent and very active creatures can move freely. If the accommodation is too small, and they do not have things to do, your pets are likely to suffer behaviour problems and stress.

Stressed chinchillas may chew their fur, display repetitive behaviours such as repeatedly back-flipping, or become aggressive to their cage mates or to people.

Ensure the accommodation is safe from other pets, such as cats, dogs and snakes, and that the chinchillas have places to hide if they feel scared.

There are a variety of chinchilla homes available in good pet stores. These should have height as well as floor space, as chinchillas love to climb. Sometimes these are made of wire mesh and are quite bare (a hangover from the fur farm design) and are not ideal. Walk-in indoor aviaries can be made into a more suitable home for your pets with plenty of room to provide:

- aerial pathways using branches from suitable types of trees that criss-cross the cage (see feeding)

- ramps

- platforms to sit on

- hayracks

- commercial mineral gnawing blocks

- cotton hammocks

- boxes to sleep in

The floor space can be used for a litter tray and also as a place to put a sand bath and tiling slabs that will provide a cool sitting spot. A breeze block will also provide a favourite look-out and resting place, and can help keep nails in trim as they clamber over it and teeth as they gnaw it.

Opposite: A Chinchilla would also benefit from somewhere to hide and more space.

Some commercial chinchilla cages have a mesh floor with a tray underneath to catch the droppings and urine. This design originates again from farms and laboratories as it is easier for us humans, but is really not pleasant for the chinchillas. Not only will they not like walking on the mesh, but they can injure their feet. As a consequence, they will spend little time on the ground, and thus have less usable space. A solid floor is much better.

Some people prefer to make their own chinchilla home. If you wish to do so, remember it needs to be chinchilla proof, and able to be cleaned easily.

The floor of your chinchillas' home will need litter to soak up urine, although they will use a litter tray if it is located in the spot they have chosen to use. Appropriate bedding and litter tray materials are products made from shredded paper, corn cobs, hardwood or bedding/litter pellets made from straw or hardwood.

Avoid products made from softwoods as these contain substances that may make your chinchilla ill. Wood shavings and sawdust are not recommended as they can cause irritation to the eyes, nose and lungs and dusty bedding can even lead to pneumonia.

It is worthwhile covering the bottom of the walls of the chinchilla's home with Plexiglas as this will help prevent litter being kicked out on to your floor by the chinchillas, thereby cutting down on the amount of cleaning you need to do!

A water bottle should be attached to the cage side at chinchilla nose height so they can easily reach it. A no-spill 'small dog' water bowl can also be provided, but be careful it does not make the bedding damp.

Opposite: Chinchillas are naturally grazing animals.

All chinchillas need access to a sand bath, ideally twice a week (see grooming). The sand bath helps clean the fur by removing excess oils and dirt. Chinchillas are very energetic and enthusiastic bathers, so bathing sand and loose fur can go flying!! Use a box with relatively high sides (25cm [10in]), or a covered cat litter tray, to help keep it contained while still being easy for your pet to get in and out of. Use fresh sand for each bath to reduce the likelihood of eye infections.

Chinchillas naturally tend to toilet in the same area most of the time, using a latrine like their wild cousins. A cat litter tray can be used for this. Watch and see where your chinchillas prefer to go to the toilet and place the litter tray there.

Finally, you may wish to provide your chinchillas with a UV light under which they can sunbathe. On a warm summer day you may wish to take your chinchillas outside in their cage in the early evening for a short period of sunbathing.

Opposite: Chinchillas love to bathe in sand.

Chinchilla proofing your home

Many chinchilla owners 'proof' a room, where the chinchillas can exercise in safety. If you let your chinchillas go free in a room, watch out for the following hazards:

- Trailing electric wires.
- Houseplants: these may be seen as a tasty snack, but are likely to be poisonous to your chinchilla.

Cover wooden furniture. For example, wrap chair and table legs in cardboard. This will stop them being chewed. Not only does this protect your furniture, but prevents your pet from accidentally eating wood that may be poisonous.

Where do I get my chinchillas from?

Getting your chinchillas from a reputable pet store may be the easiest. Your store should keep them in spacious accommodation so you will have the opportunity to watch them and make your choice. Remember they may not be too active when you visit in the day-time as that is when they normally sleep.

You could consider giving unwanted chinchillas a new home. Many pet stores now have adoption centres and, of course, there are other associations that are constantly looking to re-home unwanted pets.

If you want a particular colour that is not available at your pet store, you could try a local chinchilla rescue, or contact The National Chinchilla Society of the UK or the Mutation Chinchilla Breeders Association in America to find your nearest reputable breeder.

Signs of a healthy chinchilla

Check that the chinchillas you choose are fit and well.

Mouth

There should be no signs of dribbling, which could mean the teeth are overgrown.

Eyes

Look for bright, clear eyes, with no discharge.

Ears

Check the inside of the ears to see if they look and smell clean. There should be no sign of damage on the outer ear. There should be no sign of fungus behind the ears.

Coat

The coat should be clean and glossy, with no bald patches. A wet-looking or greasy coat suggests the chinchillas have not been well cared for and have not had access to a sand bath.

Body

The body should be well covered with muscle, with no lumps or swellings.

Tail

Check under the tail for any matting or soiling, which could indicate diarrhoea, and is a sign that the chinchilla may have tooth or intestinal problems, or is too fat.

Breathing

Watching a chinchilla's nose twitching will enable you to check its breathing, which should be quiet and regular.

Movement

Look for the typical chinchilla hop; there should be no sign of lameness.

Tameness

Ideally the chinchilla will have been gently trained to being handled by people and will be calm when picked up and held. Chinchillas that panic, run around the cage at the sight of a hand coming towards them, or try and jump to escape when picked up are going to require a lot of time and patience to persuade them that being handled by you is a relatively pleasurable experience.

Taking your chinchillas home and making friends

Ideally the chinchillas' new home should be set up and ready for them beforehand. When you first bring your chinchillas home, you will want to stroke and play with them, but you must be patient. For the first couple of days, your chinchillas need peace and quiet to get used to their new home. You will need to provide food, and change the water, so they will start getting used to you, without the stress of being handled. You could whistle gently or call their names before you put the food down. They will soon learn to come when called as they associate your whistle with something pleasant.

If you spend time getting to know your chinchillas, they will become more relaxed and want to interact with you. When they appear to be happy and settled, maybe approaching you rather than running away, then you can start making friends.

- To begin with, come close to the cage, and talk gently to your chinchillas. Do not make any sudden movements, which could alarm them.

- Offer treats so the chinchillas have to come up to see you, and get used to your hand.

Opposite: Can you speak Chinchilla?

Now try stroking your chinchillas, just before you give them a treat. Most will be happy to have their foreheads scratched. Once they are relaxed with that, you may wish to work along their head and back while you hold the treat and they nibble it. Do not be frightened if they gently nibble your finger too – it is simple curiosity and not intended to hurt. Just use one finger to begin with. Only when they are calm and relaxed should you start to use several fingers to stroke them. Remember, always, be gentle.

The next stage is to get your chinchillas out of the cage, one at a time. Be very careful, as chinchillas panic extremely easily and may be injured. They do not like being carried around, and find it very scary. After all, in nature the only time they would be carried is when they have been caught by a predator.

With one hand, scoop the chinchilla up, and with the other support its hindquarters holding its tail gently between your index and middle fingers. Bring it to your chest so that it is well supported.

As soon as the chinchilla is out of the cage, put him on the floor. When your chinchilla becomes more tame, try holding him on your lap, while you sit on the floor. Sitting on the floor with your chinchilla means he is less likely to be injured if he should wriggle or jump away.

A frightened chinchilla can move very fast and may slip his fur or deglove his tail as he wriggles out of your hands. He may be dropped or squeezed too hard as you try to hold him still. Squeezing can cause damage to the internal organs, or break his fragile rib bones.

Chinchillas will prefer being gently stroked while sitting on your lap, or next to you rather than being picked up and held.

Never turn your chinchilla on his back and stroke his tummy. He will lie very still, because this is a very scary position for chinchillas and other prey animals, such as rabbits. He will lie still because he is trying to pretend to be dead and thus of no interest to a predator. He will remain like this until he thinks the scary thing has gone away. This is a common behaviour in many small animals. Do not be fooled into thinking that he is relaxed or in a trance; research has shown that he is very alert and stressed. When the animal thinks it is safe to do so he will suddenly kick out to 'escape' and may get injured.

Other pets

If you have other pets, such as a dog or cat or ferret, you will need to be very careful, especially if you allow your chinchillas free access to areas when other pets are around. To start with, the dog should meet the chinchillas when they are safely in their cage. The chinchillas will feel frightened, so keep the dog at a distance. Reward the dog with a treat if he remains calm and well behaved.

Repeat this exercise many times until the dog loses interest in the chinchillas. But, remember, you should never allow other pets near the chinchillas without supervision. Dog, cats and ferrets are meat-eaters and the rapid movement and size of the chinchillas can easily trigger them into thinking of your chinchillas as a tasty meal.

Pictured: Take care when other pets are around.

Playtime

Chinchillas should be given the chance to behave naturally. They are gregarious and inquisitive creatures and, in the wild, would explore, socialise and forage for food.

All chinchillas should be given appropriate toys to play with and lots of hay, which they need to keep their teeth and digestive system in good order.

Once you have made friends there are many things that you and your chinchillas can do together. You may even wish to teach them tricks.

This can be a great way of bonding with your chinchillas and is lots of fun. You could even design and teach them a chinchilla agility course!!

You can help your chinchillas to live a full life by doing the following:

- Give them plenty of hay every day.

- Give them toys made of natural, untreated wood, which will be played with and chewed.

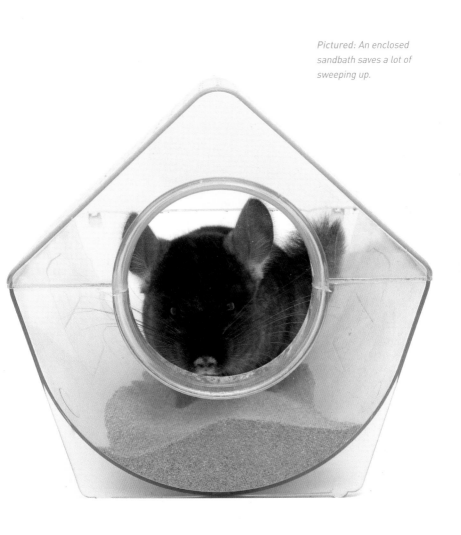

- Do not give hard, plastic toys. They may make your chinchillas very ill if they swallow a fragment.

- Make a treat box, which is a cardboard box filled with hay. You can scatter in some fresh herbs, or chinchilla food and chinchilla treats. This gives your chinchillas the chance to rummage amongst the hay, and chew up the cardboard box. A similar idea is to stuff the cardboard centres of toilet rolls with hay.

- Fill a dog activity ball with your chinchillas' daily ration of pelleted food. Your chinchillas will learn to roll the ball along to release the treats.

Puzzle feeders designed for rabbits, and toys for rats can provide a lot of fun for you and your chinchillas.

Your chinchillas may enjoy a wheel as part of their playground; ideally, a wheel each. Wheels should have solid backs and sides, but not an exposed spindle. This reduces the chances of feet or tails getting caught as the wheel spins. It should fit to the side of the cage. An alternative is the 'flying saucer' free-standing version. Whichever you choose, make sure it is big enough so that your chinchillas can move freely. If a chinchilla has to curve its spine when running in the wheel, it may do long-term damage to its back, hips and shoulders.

Pictured: Chinchillas are playful creatures.

Chinchilla behaviour

One of the most rewarding things about owning a pet is learning to understand what it is thinking or feeling. It will also help you to detect if your chinchilla is not feeling well and may need to see a vet.

If you have two or more chinchillas, you will witness natural behaviour as they interact with each other. But you can also learn a lot about an individual chinchilla by listening to the sounds it makes, and observing its body postures.

As chinchillas are most active at night, and live in dark tunnels and crevices in the daytime, they do not have a wide range of obvious body signals. Rather, most of their communication is by scent, much of which we humans cannot understand. However, they also communicate through sounds, which we can try to interpret.

Relaxed and happy chinchilla

Relaxed chinchillas are active and curious in the evening and morning, and curled up asleep by day. Chinchillas that are active a lot in the daytime are probably stressed and concerned, perhaps by sudden, unpredictable noises.

Relaxed chinchillas will just have to check everything out, to see whether it is edible, chewable or simply rather boring. Testing means nibbling. If the object is small enough, the chinchilla will take hold of it in its front paws, as you would with your hands, sit upright and give a nibble or two. If it is not of interest, the object will be dropped and the chinchilla will move on to find something else to investigate.

Opposite: How to hold your chinchilla safely.

Excited chinchillas will wave their tails as a clear signal that something of interest is happening, like you bringing their dinner!

Lookout position

The chinchilla on its hind legs, with all senses on the alert, is looking out for danger.

Frightened chinchillas

A frightened chinchilla will try to hide, making itself as small and inconspicuous as possible. However, if it is cornered and desperate it will fight and bite. Adult chinchillas that do not know each other, or no longer recognise each other as they do not smell as 'one of the group', will also fight. An additional tactic is the chinchilla 'spray gun' – a well-aimed squirt of urine. This is intended to deter the other chinchilla or the predator.

Listen to your chinchilla

Chinchillas have a wide range of sounds they make to communicate how they are feeling. These range from high-pitched squeaks to a gentle purring noise.

Soft grunts and throaty humming

A chinchilla that grunts softly or makes a humming noise in its throat is asking for attention. This can turn into rapid chirping if there is no response from its cage mate or you!

Cooing / purring

This is made by a relaxed and contented chinchilla. Your chinchilla may coo when you are gently stroking him.

Soft chirping

This is the sound made by a curious and relaxed chinchilla as it explores new objects in its home.

Alarm call

The alarm call is used to alert others in the area that danger is near. It sounds like a series of loud barks. Loud whistle-like squeaks also indicate that your chinchilla is very concerned by something it has seen, heard or smelt.

Pain and fear

A chinchilla that is in pain or very frightened will let you know by shrieking loudly and at a high pitch. This shrill noise may consist of a single shriek or several. Hopefully you will never hear your chinchillas make this noise.

Grunting

If you hear your chinchilla make a low grunt, he is not pleased with the world. It may be that he does not want to be picked up or is warning another chinchilla to leave him alone.

Teeth chattering

If grunting does not work then the chinchilla may start to click his teeth together rapidly.

He is really asking to be left alone and this sound is likely to be accompanied by the chinchilla moving away and possibly trying to hide.

Hissing and spitting

If grunting and teeth chattering have not sent a clear message to leave him alone, a chinchilla may resort to hissing and spitting to get his point across.

If you would like to hear a range of chinchilla noises you could go to the following websites

http://www.chinchilla-sounds.de/index_en.htm

http://www.cheekychinchillas.com/chinsounds.html

Food, glorious food

A well-balanced diet will keep your chinchillas healthy and will help to ensure a long life. The chinchilla digestive system is designed for a high-fibre, low-fat, low-sugar and low-protein diet. Food that is too rich or even slightly mouldy can cause serious stomach upsets, diarrhoea and even death.

In the wild, chinchillas eat grasses and plants. It is essential that chinchillas eat a lot of grass-based food, namely hay, every day. This stops their teeth growing too long and ensures their gut remains healthy. If not they can quickly suffer from gut stasis, where the guts no longer work properly, and die. Lack of hay also leads to serious and painful dental problems. Both teeth and digestive problems are common in chinchillas. They are a cause of expensive vet bills, and, sadly, often a shortened life.

Opposite: One of my Five a Day.

It is very important not to over-feed. Chinchillas can become overweight, especially if they have little to do but eat. Being overweight means they may not be able to eat their caecal pellets and become malnourished. They need the right kind of food, plenty of interesting things to play with and room to explore if they are not to become overweight and obese (see Health).

Chinchillas cannot metabolise nuts or other fatty treats. These must be avoided as they can cause hepatic lipidosis, which is a slow killer.

Hay

Chinchillas need a high level of fibre in their diet. Dried grass is available but hay is usually easier to obtain. Make sure you buy good-quality hay that smells sweet. Meadow or timothy hay is ideal. Alfalfa hay is too high in calcium and protein for chinchillas to have as their basic diet, but a little as a treat will be enjoyed. Do not feed hay that is dusty or mouldy.

Hay should be available to your chinchillas at all times and should be the main part of their diet.

Vegetables and fruit

Chinchillas love fresh vegetables and fruit. The best plan is to introduce one at a time so that they get used to it and do not get an upset stomach from a sudden change in diet.

Opposite: Hay is an essential part of the daily diet.

A teaspoon or so of fresh food per individual adult chinchilla every day is enough for them to enjoy and not risk getting a gassy, bloated stomach or diarrhoea.

Chinchilla favourites include raisins, apple, blueberries, grapes, orange, pumpkin, squash, sweet potatoes, fresh herbs and flowers.

Avoid seeds, nuts, leafy vegetables such as cabbage, broccoli and spinach, beans, peas and salad vegetables including tomatoes, lettuce and cucumber. These can trigger serious digestive upsets and diarrhoea.

When giving any fresh food to your pet it is important to make sure it is rinsed well under cold water to clean away any dirt or insects. You should never feed any fruit or vegetable that is over or under-ripe or that is wilting, as this is not healthy for your chinchillas. A good rule of thumb to follow is: would you eat it? If not, then do not feed it to your pet.

Never collect fresh plants from the side of the road or from areas that have been, or are likely to have been, sprayed with pesticides as this will cause harm to your pets. Many plants are poisonous to chinchillas, so be aware. Likewise, never feed grass cuttings from the lawn mower, as these may be contaminated with exhaust fumes or metal particles.

Instead, try to grow your own fresh herbs. These can include peppermint, lemon-balm, and chamomile. Other treats which your chinchillas will love are breadsticks, rusks and twigs of trees such as birch, hazel, willow, beech and apple. You can leave the leaves on, though it is a good idea to dry them. Again, make sure the tree has not been treated with pesticides and wash the twigs before giving them to your pets.

Complementary diets – supplementary feeding

There are a number of commercial diets that are specially made for chinchillas, which contain the nutrients needed to keep them healthy – including calcium for strong, healthy tooth growth.

Because chinchillas are naturally 'fussy' eaters, known as selective feeders, mixed diets that resemble human muesli breakfast cereals are not the best. The chinchillas will tend to pick out certain items, particularly the sweeter ingredients, and leave the rest. Thus they do not get a balanced diet and may end up with health problems and obesity issues.

Though it may look less interesting to us, a better choice is a good quality pelleted food designed for chinchillas.

Commercial pellets, or muesli type food, should be fed sparingly. Overfeeding of such diets can lead to problems with teeth and intestines, obesity, and boredom and aggression. As a rough guide, a teaspoon a day for an adult chinchilla is enough, the rest of the diet being hay and a little bit of fruit and vegetables.

It is very easy to overfeed commercial diets, so do take care.

How much?

Chinchillas are grazers, eating throughout the time they are awake. Hay should always be available for them to nibble. Vegetables and their ration of commercial diet can be given once a day or split over two feeding times.

As a rough guide 80% of your chinchillas' diet should be hay, 10% fresh vegetables and 10% pellet or muesli-type chinchilla food.

Opposite: Remember the outside run needs a roof.

Chinchilla care

Looking after chinchillas means keeping their house clean and being on the lookout for health problems.

Many chinchillas live a shortened life because their owners do not understand chinchilla needs and may not provide a suitable diet and adequate accommodation.

Opposite: Look after me and I will be your friend for a long time.

Daily tasks

- Remove all uneaten food and wash the bowls. If you frequently find uneaten food in the bowls it may mean you are feeding too much, so give them less next time. But do check that your chinchilla is eating and is not unwell.

- Refill the water-bottle with fresh water. Check that your chinchilla is drinking from the bottle - if not it may be that he is ill. If chinchillas do not drink frequently they can quickly become constipated and dehydrated.

- Refill the hayrack with fresh hay.

- Remove wet bedding and droppings, checking as you do that the droppings look healthy.

- Check your chinchilla's rear end to ensure it is clean.

Chinchillas do not need to be groomed; indeed, brushing can damage their fur. However, they do need a sand bath at least twice a week, but more frequently can lead to eye problems and an over dry coat. The bath is in dry sand, not water. In the high mountains where they naturally live, they clean their fur by rolling around in fine sand. The sand then gets into the coat, cleaning away dirt and grease as it does so. A few quick shakes afterwards leaves the coat clean and the fur fluffy.

It is important that chinchillas are able to keep their coats clean, as the dense fine fur can quickly become matted. This can lead to sores on the skin and generally being unwell. If you handle you chinchilla when your hands are hot and sweaty or if the conditions are hot and humid, remember your chinchillas will need a sand bath to keep themselves clean and fresh.

A sand bath is a simple bowl or other container that enables the chinchilla to roll thoroughly around in the fine, dusty sand. This must be an appropriate type sold for chinchillas, such as ground pumice stone or silver sand. Do not use builders sand or that used for children's' sandpits. Use fresh sand for each bath to reduce the likelihood of eye infections and irritation. Never bathe your chinchillas in water.

Weekly tasks

- Clean the cage thoroughly, using an animal friendly disinfectant.

- Remove all bedding, put some of it to one side and throw the rest away.

- Remove all litter from the litter tray, clean the tray, and replace with fresh litter.

- Clean the water bottle.

- Put in the new bedding and the bit of old bedding you kept to one side. This means your chinchillas will feel safe when you put them back in their home as it will have a familiar scent.

Give each of your chinchillas an all-over health check (see Health section).

- Check your chinchillas' teeth, and run your fingers gently along the jaw line to check for any bumps.

- Check your chinchillas' nails.

- Check inside the ears to ensure that they are clean, and then sniff for any unusual or pungent odour, which could indicate infection or other problems. Do not try and clean the ears with a cotton bud! Dirty ears need treating by a vet.

- Check the underside of your chinchillas' feet for any sores.

- Check their fur for any fur loss

- Weigh your chinchillas to check they are not losing or gaining weight.

Health

Handling your pet every day and performing regular health checks will help you pick up on the early signs of ill health and take action quickly to treat ailments before they become too serious. This is best done while handling your pet in the normal way. You should do any examinations as part of your stroking and regular play.

You should know how your pet behaves while healthy. A change in normal patterns of behaviour can indicate ill health. These include being less active, being wobbly, changes in eating or drinking habits, over grooming, hiding more or becoming aggressive.

Chinchillas are prey animals and are very good at disguising signs of illness, so familiarity with your own pets is vital. As a guide, signs of a ill health can include a greasy coat, sitting still with a hunched body, faded, dull or bulging eyes.

If your chinchilla is less active than normal he may be unwell.

Faeces are an important sign, and cage droppings should be checked daily. Normal droppings should be the size of a large grain of rice, hard, dry, dark brown and slightly shiny. Any change in the number or texture of droppings should cause concern, especially if the stools are loose or fewer in number. It is important that you contact your vet as soon as possible if you see any of these signs. Chinchillas that are ill can deteriorate quickly and their condition can become very serious, even fatal, within just a few hours.

Weigh your chinchillas weekly and remember to keep a record of their weight. Once they are full grown it should remain constant. Even half an ounce up or down in weight can indicate that all is not well. A set of kitchen scales work well if they have a deep weighing bowl in which your pet can sit safely. You can train each of your chinchillas to sit quietly in the bowl by luring it in with a small treat, such as a quarter of a raisin. As it gets used to doing this, slowly lengthen the time between getting in the bowl and getting the treat.

Accidents, injuries or illness can occur and in the first instance a vet should be contacted to arrange treatment. But, in the time between the discovery of a problem and reaching the surgery, you are responsible for providing the best care you can.

Whether you are going to the vet for a check-up or because your pet is ill, take your chinchilla in a secure box, such as a sturdy plastic cat carrier.

Ideally, when you go to the vet take all your chinchillas with you. Chinchillas recognise each other by scent, and it is important that they share the same scent profile if they are to be reintroduced successfully after they have been separated. If you cannot take the chinchillas together, ask your veterinary surgeon for advice on scent swapping before you reintroduce them.

Wounds

Stress is the main cause of wounds. Fighting between cage-mates is not common but can be an indicator of several types of stressor. Stressed chinchillas may chew and pull out their own fur or that of their cage-mate. Bald or patchy fur may indicate diet issues, environmental stress or problems between the cage mates, especially if they are males.

Injuries to the eyes can be serious, though rare, but accidents do happen especially if a frightened chinchilla is moving rapidly. A saline (rock salt and water) wash to flush the eye and release any foreign bodies is worthwhile, carefully done using a pipette.

You should contact your veterinary surgeon at once if the eye is held closed or appears opaque.

Broken Bones

Chinchillas are curious, active and easily frightened. They have fragile bones, which can break easily. If you believe your pet has suffered a broken bone, telephone your vet immediately.

Teeth

Keep a very close check on your chinchillas' teeth to make sure they do not grow too long or become mis-aligned. Such problems can indicate an inappropriate diet, or an injury, abscess or illness.

Chinchilla teeth grow quickly. If your chinchilla has damp fur under his chin, is drooling, or having difficulty eating (this is one reason to check his weight weekly), the teeth may need to be filed down or even removed. In the worst cases, tooth root abscesses can develop and the condition can become intractable. Long term treatment, needing repeated anaesthetics and dental operations may be required. Even then, secondary abscesses and bone infection may result. Many chinchillas with advanced dental disease have to be euthanized.

Your chinchillas are less likely to develop problems if they have lots of hay to eat, enabling them to wear down their teeth naturally.

Throat Blockage

Chinchillas may suffer a throat blockage if they swallow something too large, such as a nut, without chewing it first. Chewing non-food items such as carpets, wires and plastic may also lead to blockages. These will be indicted by the chinchilla retching and drooling. The object will need to be removed by a vet.

Bloat

Bloat occurs when there is a build-up of gas in the stomach and the bowel, typically the caecum. It can be fatal. It can be caused by a wide variety of things including stress, dental problems, a blockage caused by swallowing a non-food item or a sudden change in diet. The most obvious signs of bloat are a swollen hard stomach, lack of appetite, lethargy and dehydration. Veterinary advice should be sought immediately. Collapse and death can occur quickly.

Diarrhoea

If you notice that your chinchilla is not eating, drinking or there is any change in the size or consistency of its droppings then you must contact a vet. These changes should be taken very seriously as they can have a number of causes and can rapidly be fatal. They can be caused by a poor diet, pain or an illness. It may also mean your chinchilla has eaten something poisonous. Chinchillas are unable to vomit and so everything they eat has to go through the whole gut. Consult your vet for advice and treatment.

Pictured: An example of a Chinchilla looking stressed.

Heatstroke

Chinchillas can overheat very quickly and fatally. Prevention, by ensuring your pets have access to cool stones or tiles to lie on, is the best policy. If the weather is very hot, then provide chew-proof 'ice bottles' such as frozen tins of food or a stainless steel water bottle filled and cooled in the freezer. These must be wrapped in a towel to prevent any freezer burn and to keep them cool longer. A fan that is faced away from the chinchillas' home can help cool the air in the room without causing draughts.

Nails

In the wild, a chinchilla would keep its nails in trim by running and climbing over the rocky ground. A pet chinchilla's nails may grow too long, which will make moving very uncomfortable as they can curve over and dig into the feet or distort the toes. Placing some rougher surfaces in your chinchillas' home can help keep their nails in good condition.

A simple way is to put in a few concrete paving stones, breeze blocks or a brick platform that they can walk and climb on. Putting their vegetables and pellets on this means they will have to walk on the rough surface, which will help wear the nails.

Bumblefoot

This is an extremely painful condition and is characterised by the feet being swollen and blistered, which can turn into open pressure sores. Infections from such sores can spread to the bones of the feet. This is often caused by having wire floors in the cage. If you see any swellings on the feet, do contact your vet.

Opposite: Curious but cautious.

Ears

Chinchillas rarely get ear infections, but may pick up ear mites. If you see your chinchilla scratching its ear more than normal, or even tilting its head on one side, it may mean there are mites and a trip to the vet is called for.

Do not try and clean the ears with a cotton bud! Dirty ears need treating by a vet.

Opposite: Check your chinchilla's ears regularly.

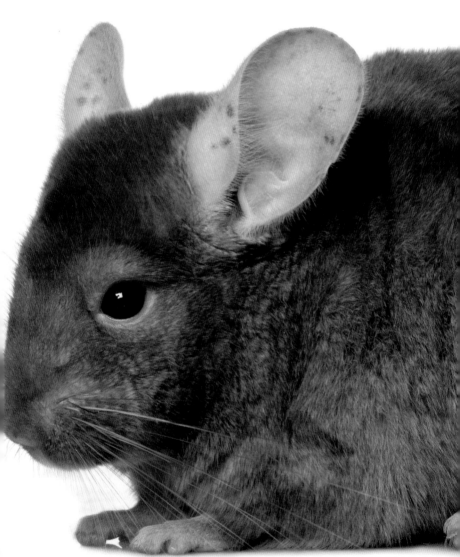

Chinchilla medicine

Veterinary knowledge of chinchillas has increased hugely over the last few years and now there is much more that can be done for your pet. However, unlike cat and dog medicine, which all veterinary surgeons know a lot about, chinchillas are a specialist subject. They are considered an exotic species in terms of veterinary care. It is well worth finding a vet who is interested in chinchillas and their treatment, and may even have a qualification in exotic animal medicine.

Know your
pet chinchilla

Scientific name	Chinchilla lanigera
Group order	Rodentia
Lifespan	10 – 20 years
Size	600g (1.3lb.)
Gestation	111 days
Litter size	2 - 3 (average)
Birth weight	40 g (1.4 oz.) approx.
Birth type	fully furred, eyes open, mobile
Weaning	6 - 9 weeks
Breeding age	
Female	6 - 8 months
Male	5 - 6 months

Hold your chinchilla
close to your body,
support its weight
and gently hold its tail
between your fingers.

Sources of Further Information

Training Chinchillas

Orr, J and Lewin, T 2005 Getting Started: clicking with your rabbit Karen Pryor Publications

Orr, J and Lewin, T. Clicker Train your small pet http://www.clickerbunny.com/article_clickercritter.htm

Pryor, K. How to clicker train your critter http://www.clickertraining.com/node/3226

Showing Chinchillas:

National Chinchilla Society (UK) www.natchinsoc.co.uk

Mutation Chinchilla Breeders Association (USA) www.mutationchinchillas.com

Wild Chinchillas:

www.iucnredlist.org International Union for Conservation of Nature and Natural Resources (IUCN) is the world's main authority on the state of the plants and animals with whom we share our world and the Red List is a summary of those species under serious threat of extinction. The aim of the Red List is to convey the urgency and scale of conservation problems to the public and policy makers, and to motivate the global community to try to reduce species extinctions.

www.wildchinchilla.org Save the Wild Chinchillas is a conservation organization aiming to restore essential habitat for endangered Chilean chinchillas while deterring further habitat degradation. The main objectives are to educate and involve people worldwide in conservation, promote habitat regeneration, and create a knowledge base. Since 1996, they have created and distributed educational materials ranging from children's stories to scientific publications with the help of artists, students, teachers, scientists, and zoos internationally. They work directly with the local community, focusing on creating and enhancing habitat for chinchillas on communal lands.

Weights & measures

If you prefer your units in pounds and inches, you can use this conversion chart:

Length in inches	Length in cm	Weight in kg	Weight in lbs
1	2.5	0.5	1.1
2	5.1	0.7	1.5
3	7.6	1	2.2
4	10.2	1.5	3.3
5	12.7	2	4.4
8	20.3	3	6.6
10	25.4	4	8.8
15	38.1	5	11

Measurements rounded to 1 decimal place.